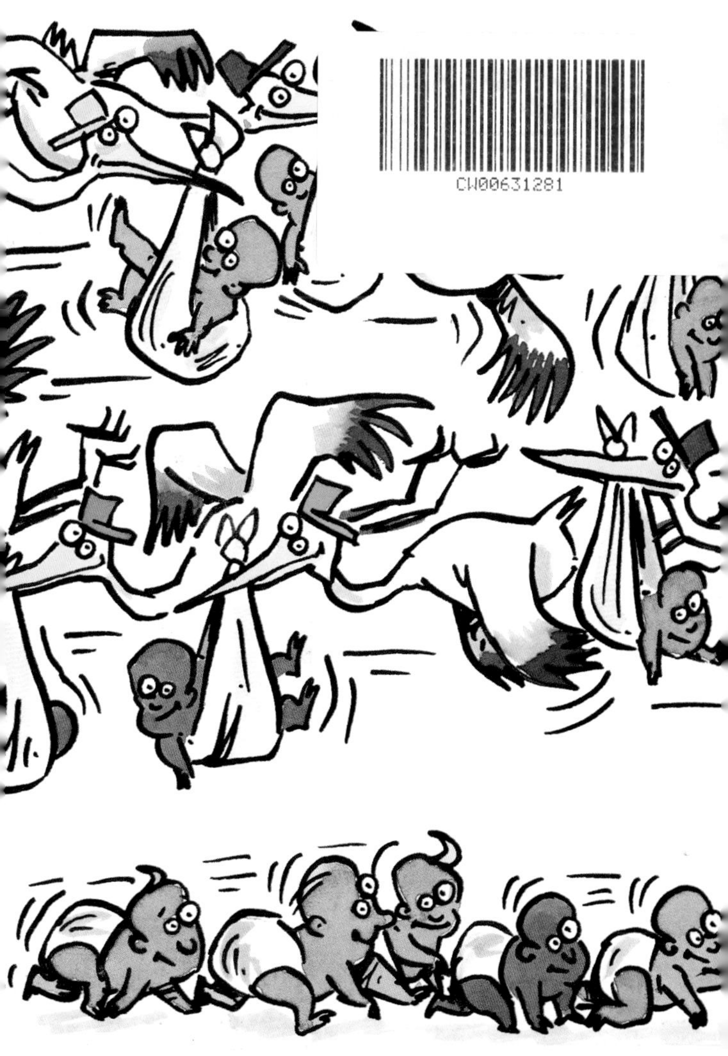

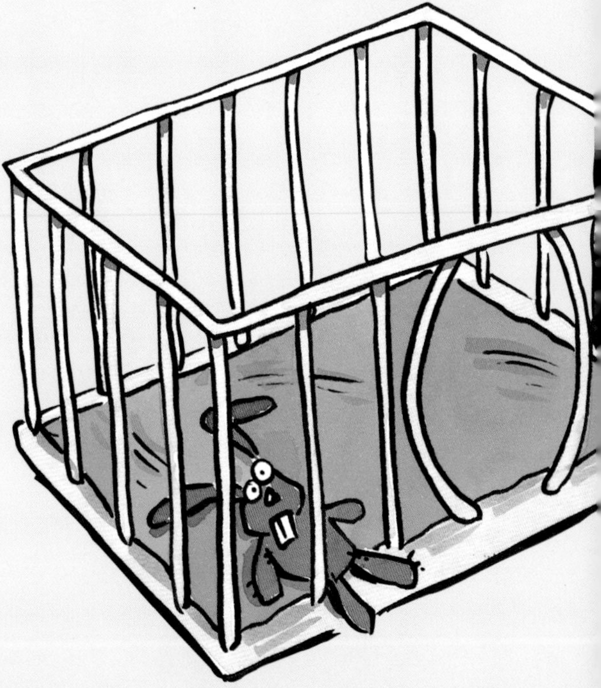

TOO STRONG

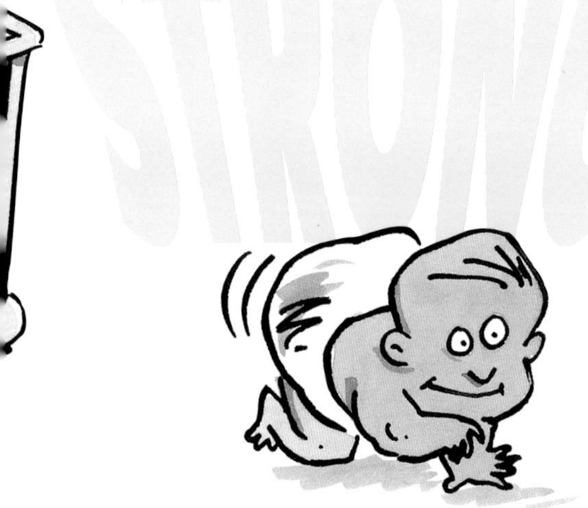

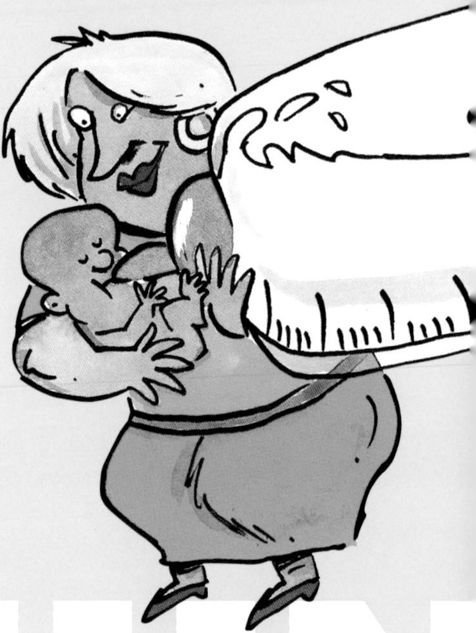

Too
HUN

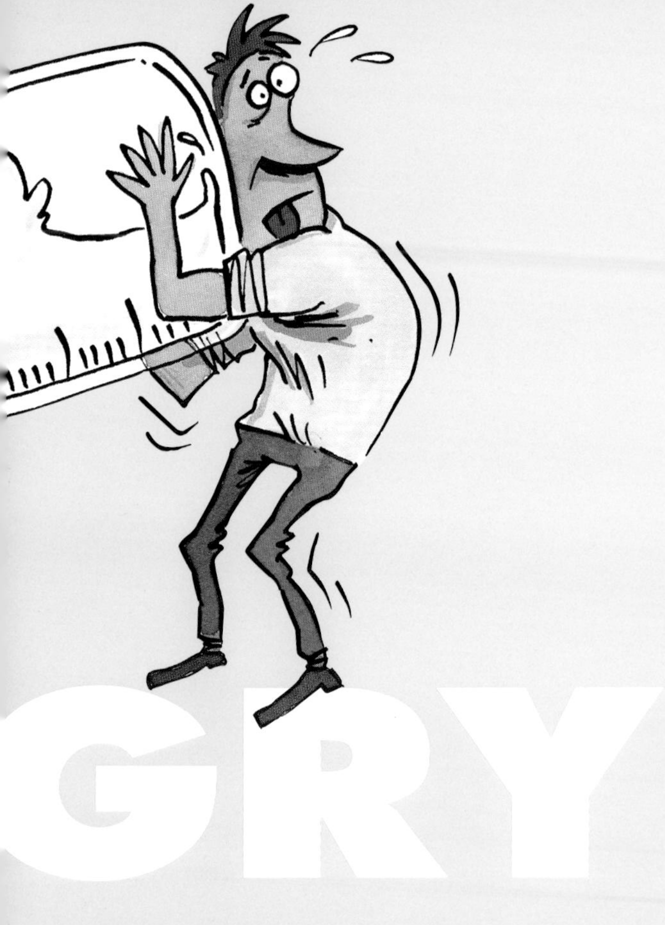
GRY

Too smelly

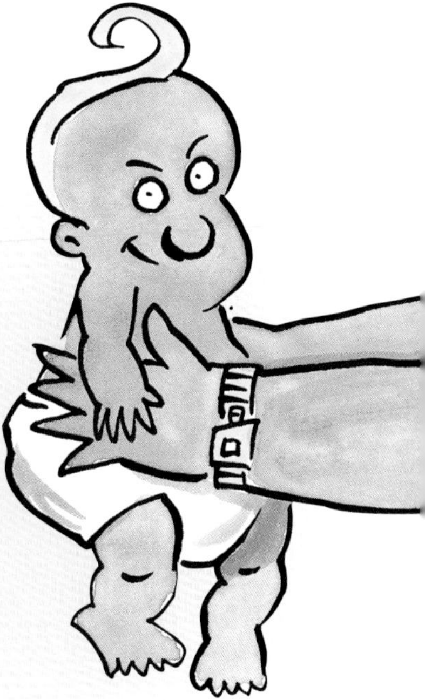

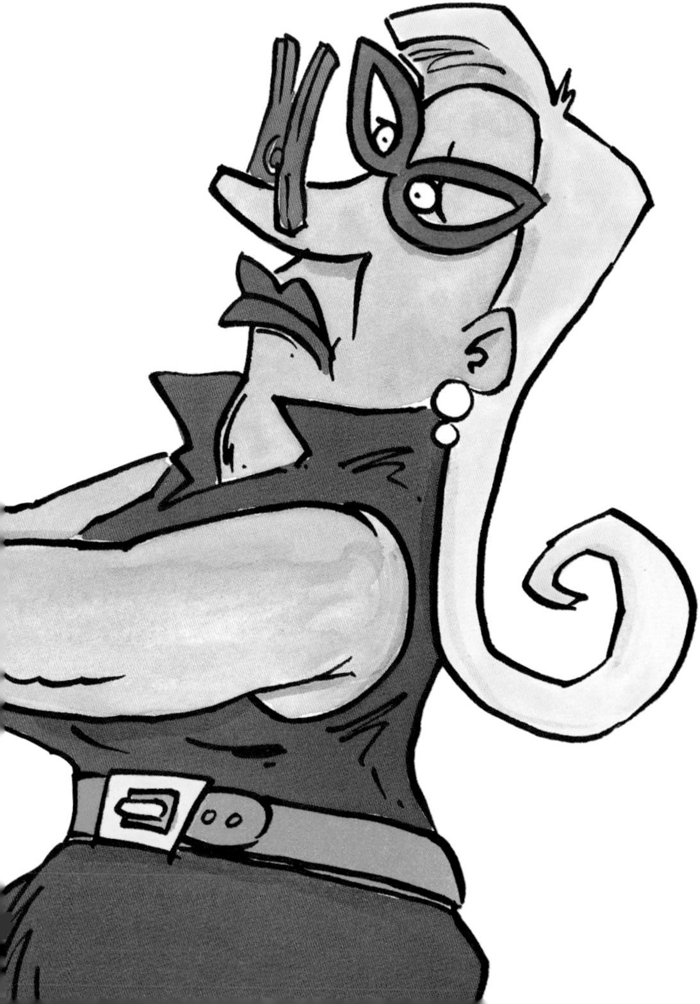

TOO MESSY

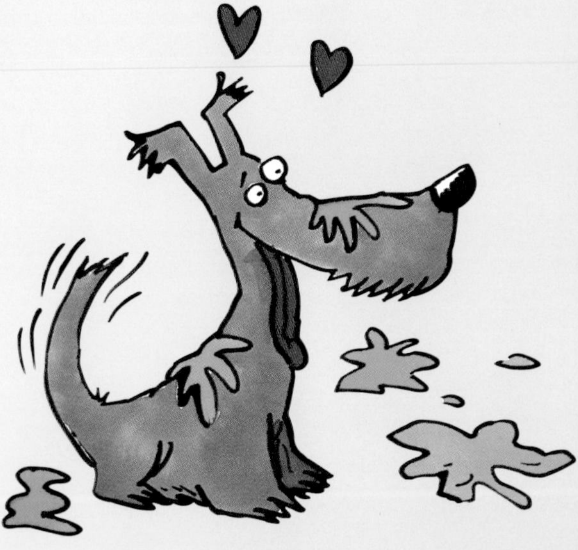

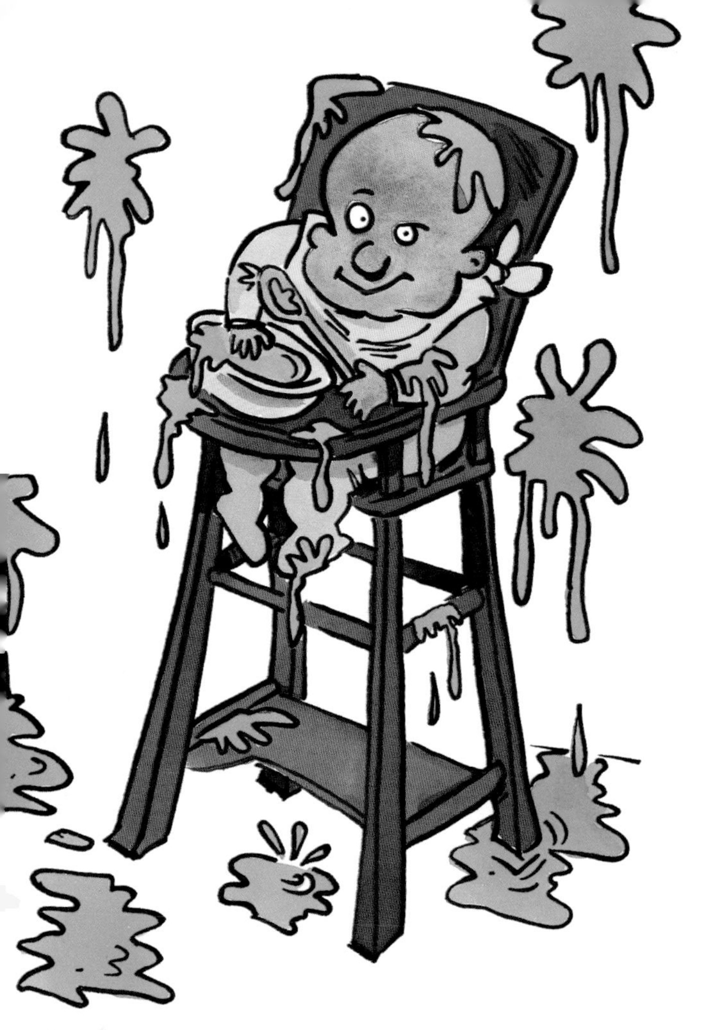

Too noisy . . .

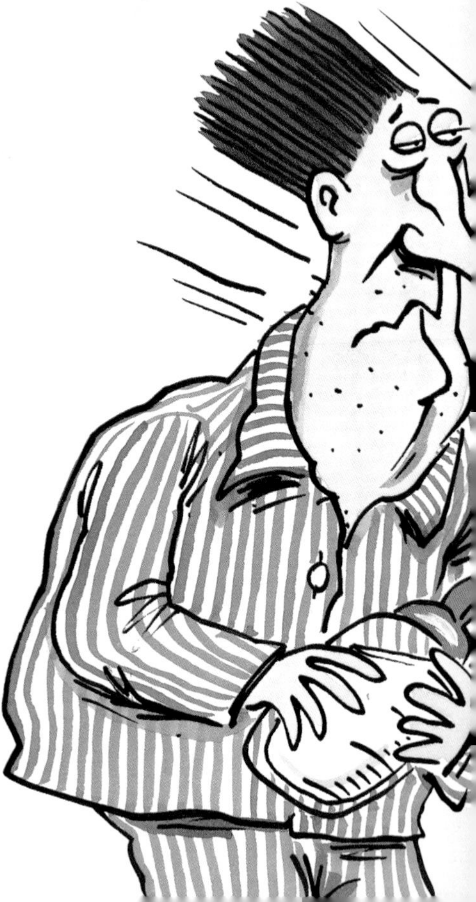

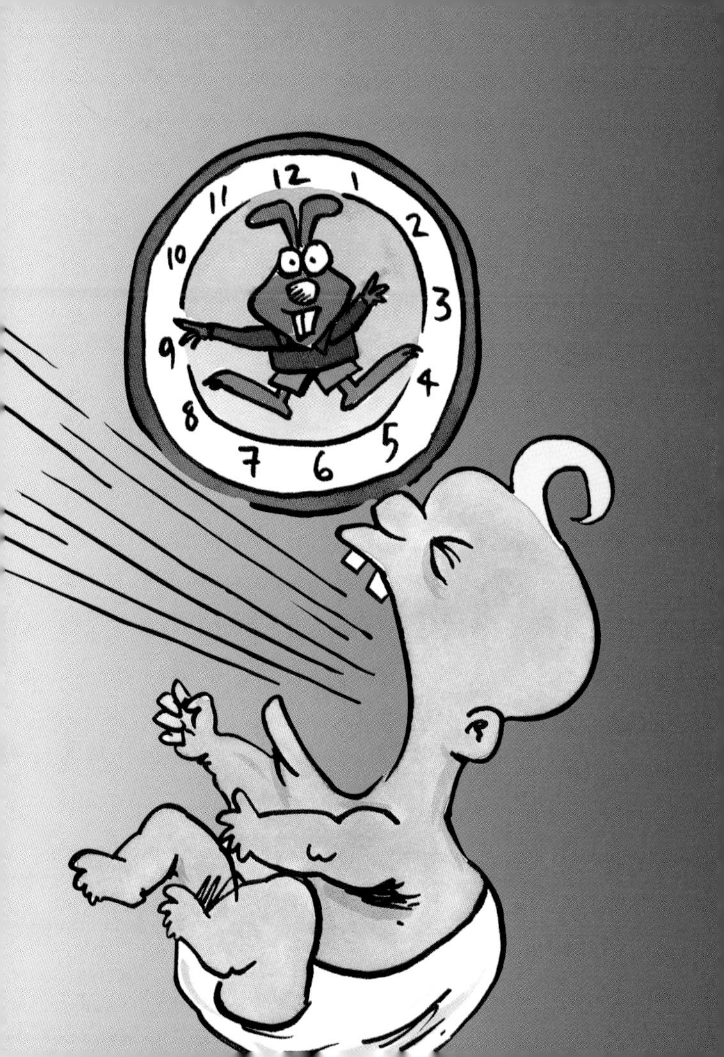

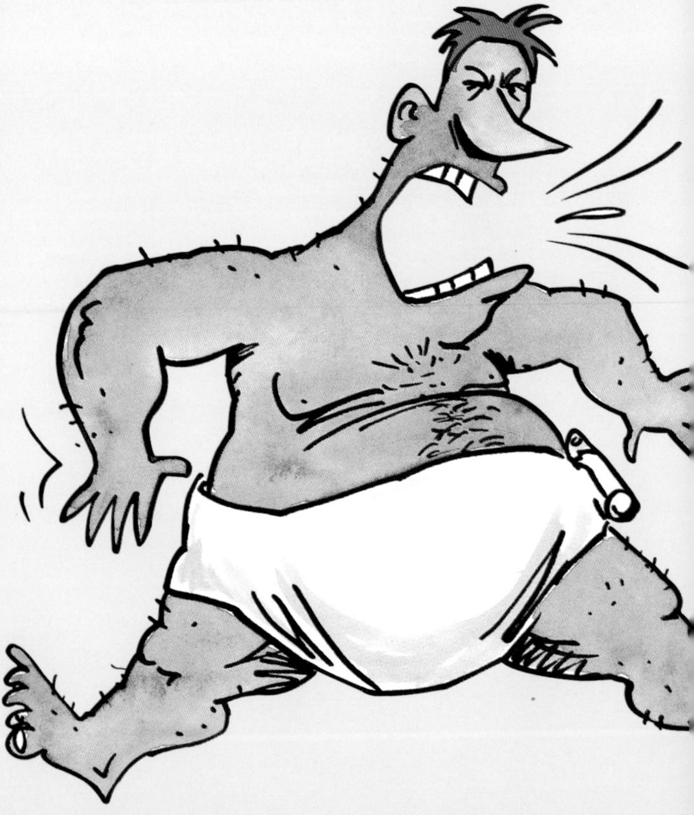

Too BIG

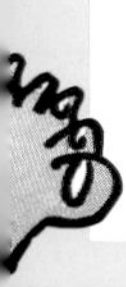

Too dribbly

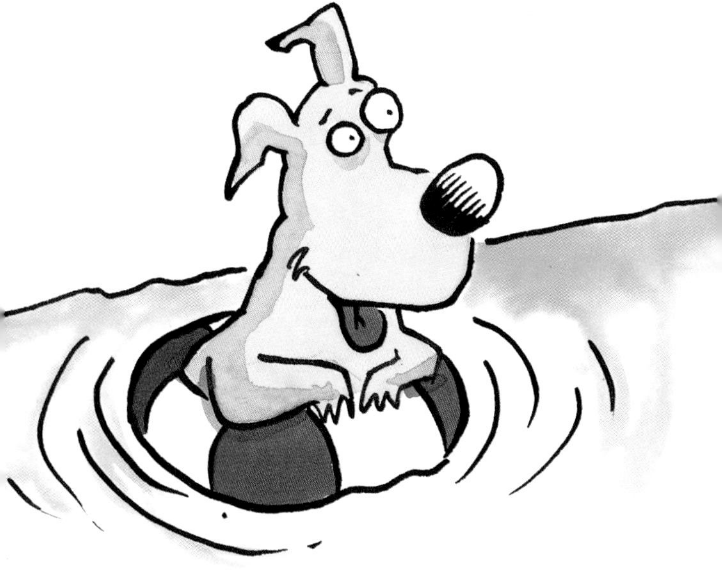

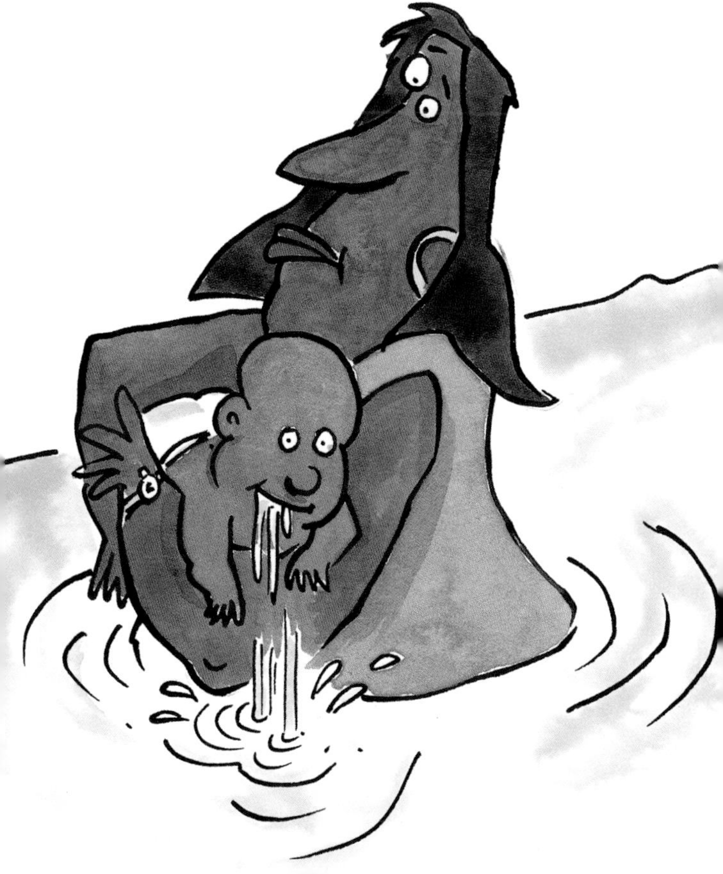

. . . still too noisy!

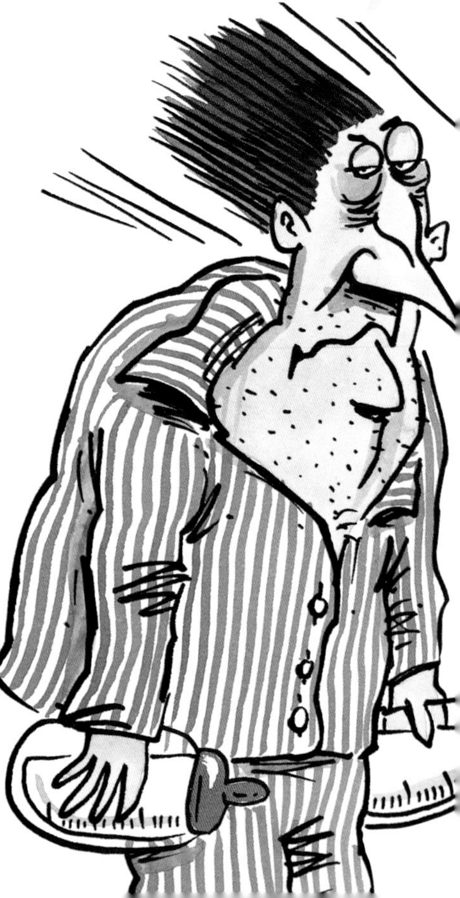

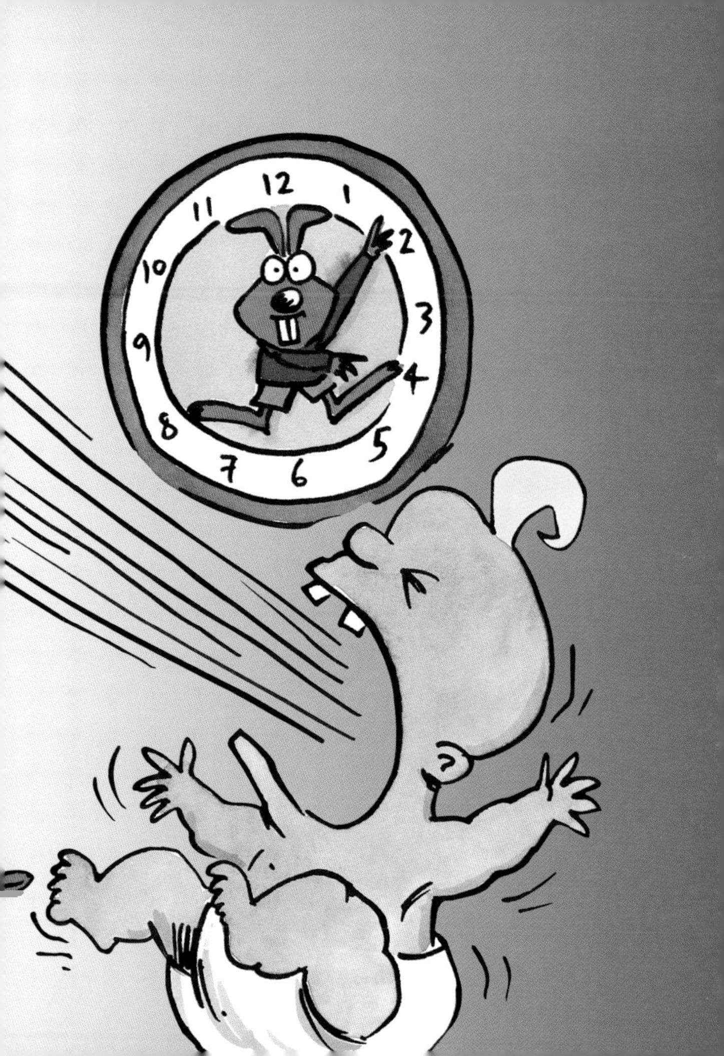

Just right!

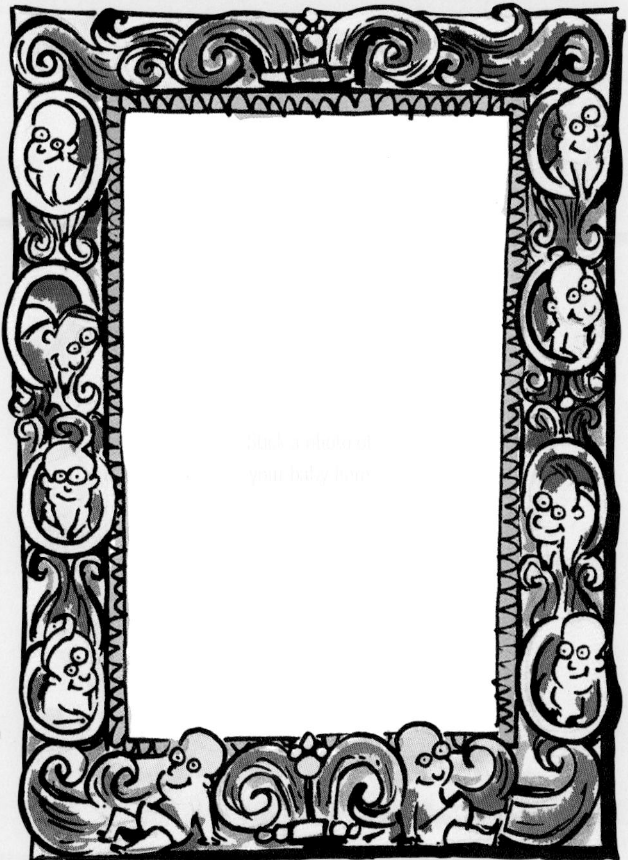
Stick a photo of
your baby here

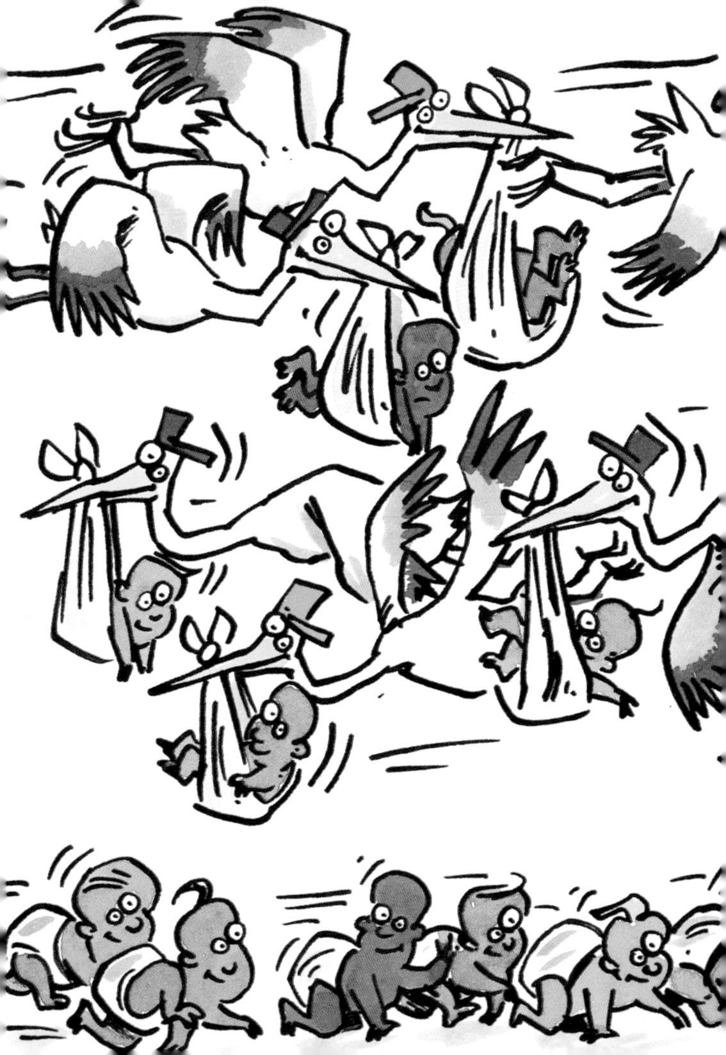